We hope you enjoy *That's a Good Tune* Book 2
for C and B♭ instruments and piano.
Further copies of this and the other books in the series
are available from your local music shop.

In case of difficulty, please contact the publisher direct:

The Sales Department
KEVIN MAYHEW LTD
Rattlesden
Bury St Edmunds
Suffolk IP30 0SZ

Phone 01449 737978
Fax 01449 737834

Please ask for our complete catalogue of outstanding Instrumental Music.

First published in Great Britain in 1995 by Kevin Mayhew Ltd

© Copyright 1995 Kevin Mayhew Ltd

ISBN 0 86209 623 5
Catalogue No: 3611150

The arrangements in this book are protected by copyright
and may not be reproduced in any way for sale or private use
without the consent of the copyright owner.

Front cover design by Roy Mitchell
Music Editor: Anthea Smith
Music setting by Louise Hill

Printed and bound in Great Britain

CONTENTS

		Page	
		Score	*Part*
Blues for a Pink Elephant	Harry Rabinowitz	10	3
Charlie's Cakewalk	Betty Roe	23	8
Dapper Duke	John Dankworth	8	2
Hippy Habanera	Betty Roe	12	4
Hot, Buttered Toast	Richard Lloyd	18	6
How do you do?	Andrew Moore	21	8
Jim Knobbly Knees	Max Harris	15	5
Jonty's Jaunt	Norman Warren	28	10
Lost Lullaby	Andrew Gant	31	11
March of the Monkeys	Malcolm Archer	19	7
Mind the Dog	Mike Sammes	16	6
The Alligator Stomp	Colin Mawby	26	10
What a Surprise	Mike Sammes	13	4
Windscreen Wiper Waltz	Christopher Tambling	7	2

About the Composers

Malcolm Archer, sometime cocktail bar pianist, is an international organist and recently gave a recital on the largest organ in the world at Wanamaker's Department Store in Philadelphia. He appears frequently on the BBC2 programme *The Organist Entertains* and was organ soloist on the recording *Classic Rock Symphonies* with the London Symphony Orchestra.

John Dankworth is the ultimate all-round musician: jazzman playing with all the greatest names from Dizzy Gillespie to Sarah Vaughan; prolific composer of film scores, choral and orchestral works; conductor of symphony orchestras worldwide; and educationalist. In addition to all this he has the good fortune to be married to the singer Cleo Laine.

Andrew Gant is a singer, pianist, conductor and arranger, working with such famous vocal groups as The Tallis Scholars, The Sixteen and the choir of Westminster Abbey. He is musical director of the Light Blues, with whom he has toured all over the world, and the Thursford Christmas concerts which regularly attract an audience of over 70,000. And, if that's not a busy enough life, he is also Director of Music in Chapel at Selwyn College, Cambridge.

Max Harris has won two Ivor Novello awards for *The Gurney Slade* theme and *The Kipling Stories* theme. He is also the composer of numerous other theme tunes, including *Porridge, Open All Hours* and *Poldark 2*. As musical director he was responsible for several LP's featuring Yehudi Menuhin and Stephane Grapelli.

Richard Lloyd had a youthful ambition to be a (respectable) night club pianist in Paris. When that didn't work out he became Organist of Durham Cathedral instead, and has since followed a distinguished career as a church musician and composer of choral music. He is especially interested in writing music for young players.

Colin Mawby is choral director of RTE, the Irish radio and television station. He has conducted many of the finest choirs and orchestras including the BBC Singers, the Belgian Radio Choir and the London Mozart Players. On the lighter side of music, he has worked with U2 and appeared in multi-media events with many popular artists. He is a prolific composer.

Andrew Moore learned his first music from his father, a jazz pianist in the style of Art Tatum with Jack Jackson's Band. He studied violin, organ and conducting at the Royal Academy of Music and is now a Benedictine Monk of Downside Abbey.

Harry Rabinowitz – 'what a troublesome surname', he says – was born in South Africa and came to England to study. His career, via the BBC and ITV, has developed into composing for TV and films and conducting serious concerts and pop festivals in several cities, notably London, Los Angeles and Boston. These are his first, and very enjoyable to compose, pieces for young people.

Betty Roe is a cabaret artiste, wizz piano player and composer. She studied at the Royal Academy of Music and later with the famous British composer Lennox Berkeley. Her musicals for schools bear her trade marks of wit and humour.

Mike Sammes is the founder of the famous Mike Sammes singers, who have worked with hundreds of major artists including Cliff Richard, Andy Williams, The Beatles, Tom Jones, Barbara Streisand – the list is endless. They have also issued a string of successful solo albums of their own and were recently awarded BASCA's Gold Badge for services to British music.

Christopher Tambling is Director of Music at Glenalmond College in Perth, Scotland. He plays organ and harpsichord and conducts the Perth Symphony Orchestra. When he is not composing he likes to cook and make wine. His recent musical *Singing, Dancing Carpenter*, co-authored with Michael Forster, is enjoying enormous success.

Norman Warren used to play the great Wurlitzer organ at the Trocadero in London's Elephant and Castle (he was paid ten shillings a session – fifty pence in today's money) and he once played for Diana Dors. Now, as Archdeacon of Rochester, he is more concerned with church organs and is a prolific composer of hymns and choral music.

For Sara

WINDSCREEN WIPER WALTZ

CHRISTOPHER TAMBLING

© Copyright 1995 by Kevin Mayhew Ltd.
It is illegal to photocopy music.

DAPPER DUKE

JOHN DANKWORTH

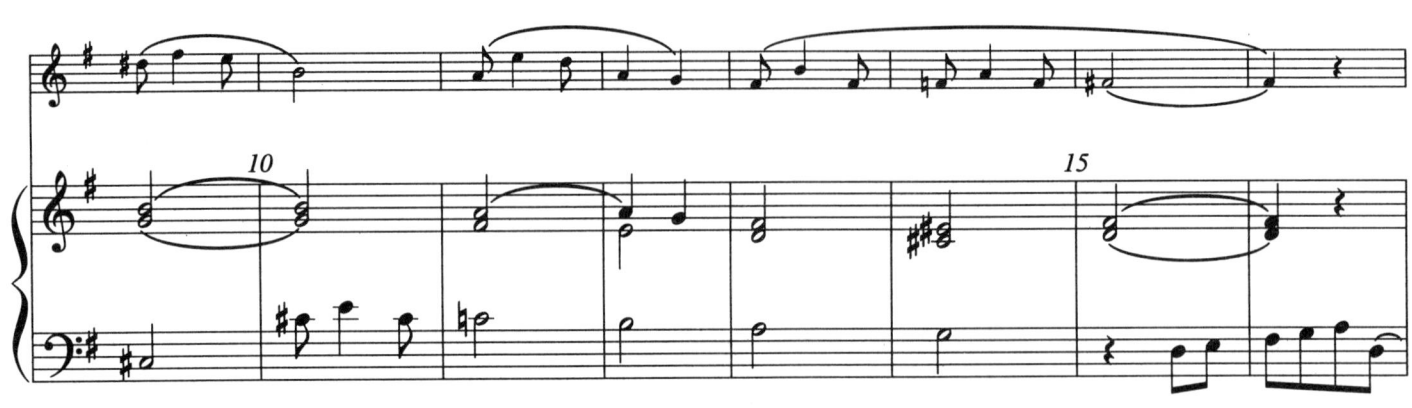

© Copyright 1995 by Kevin Mayhew Ltd.
It is illegal to photocopy music.

BLUES FOR A PINK ELEPHANT

HARRY RABINOWITZ

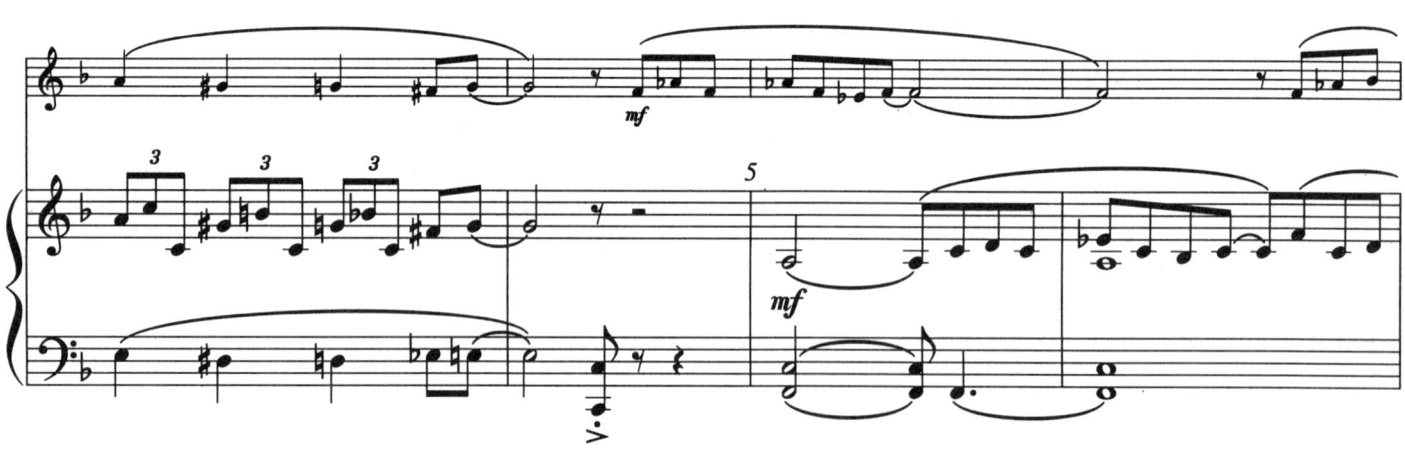

The quavers in this piece should be swung so that ♫ becomes ♩♪

© Copyright 1995 by Kevin Mayhew Ltd.
It is illegal to photocopy music.

For Sarah

HIPPY HABANERA

BETTY ROE

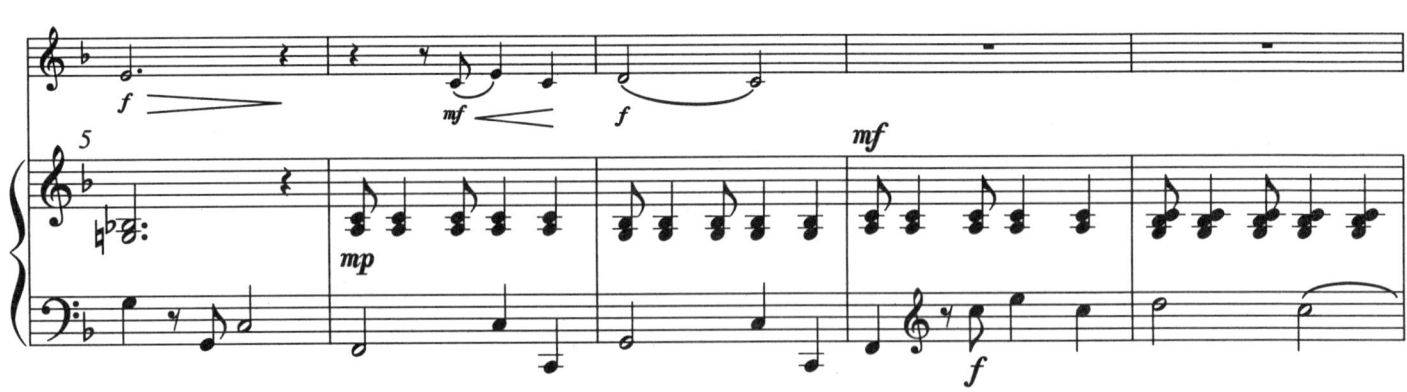
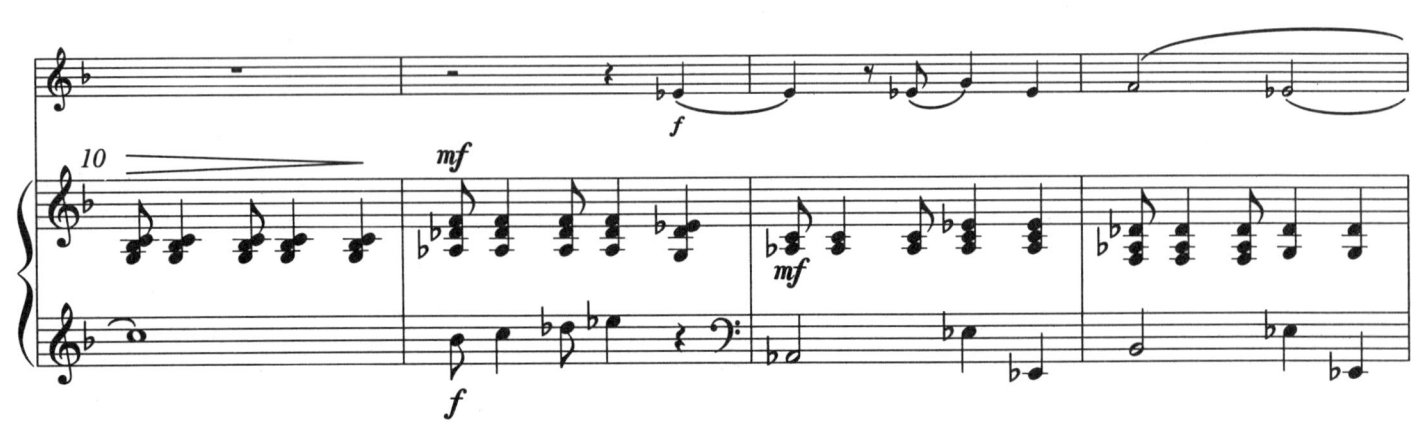

© Copyright 1995 by Kevin Mayhew Ltd.
It is illegal to photocopy music.

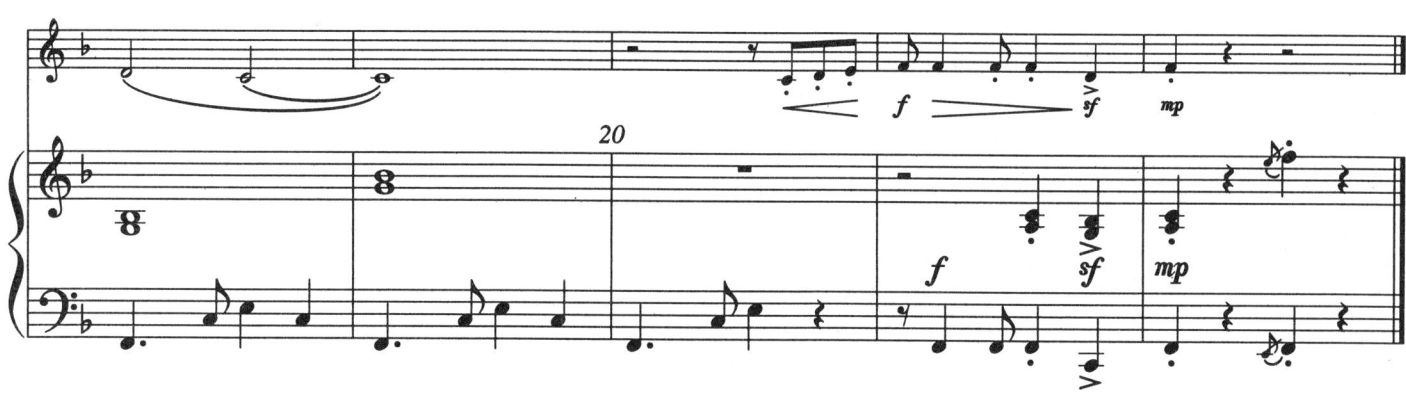

WHAT A SURPRISE

MIKE SAMMES

© Copyright 1995 by Kevin Mayhew Ltd.
It is illegal to photocopy music.

13

JIM KNOBBLY KNEES

MAX HARRIS

© Copyright 1995 by Kevin Mayhew Ltd.
It is illegal to photocopy music.

MIND THE DOG
MIKE SAMMES

© Copyright 1995 by Kevin Mayhew Ltd.
It is illegal to photocopy music.

HOT, BUTTERED TOAST

RICHARD LLOYD

MARCH OF THE MONKEYS

MALCOLM ARCHER

© Copyright 1995 by Kevin Mayhew Ltd.
It is illegal to photocopy music.

Kevin Mayhew

For Sara

WINDSCREEN WIPER WALTZ

CHRISTOPHER TAMBLING

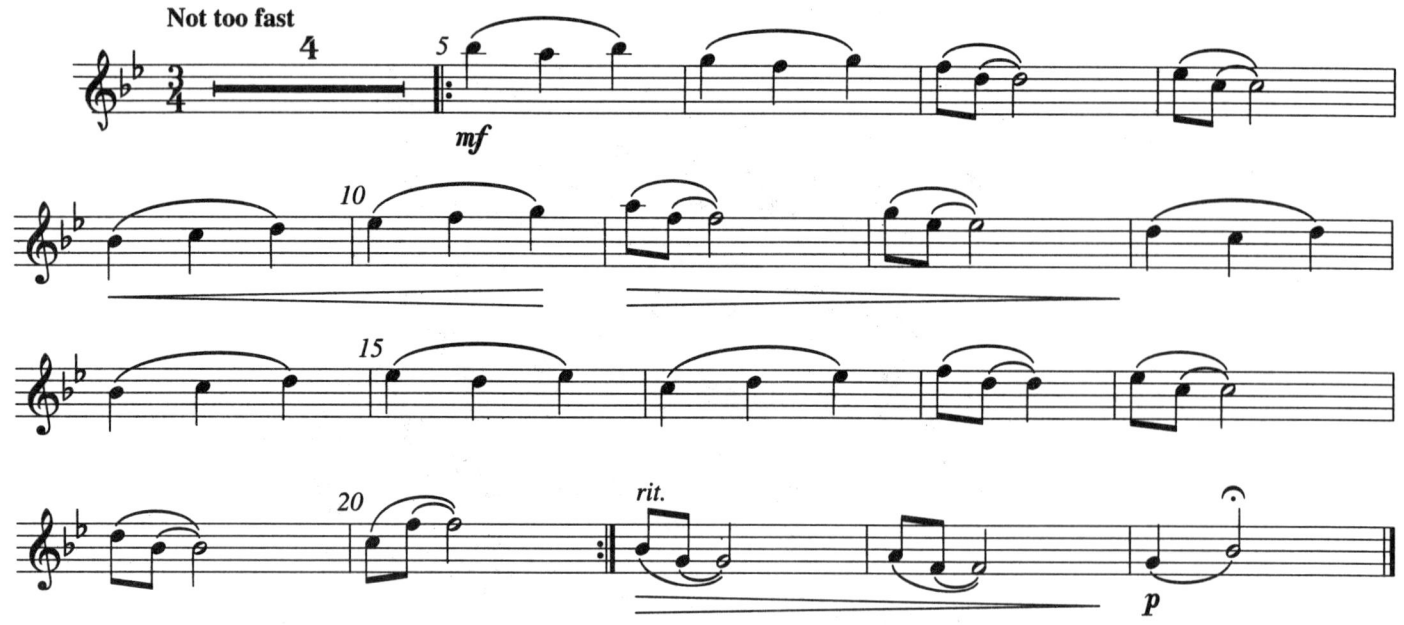

DAPPER DUKE

JOHN DANKWORTH

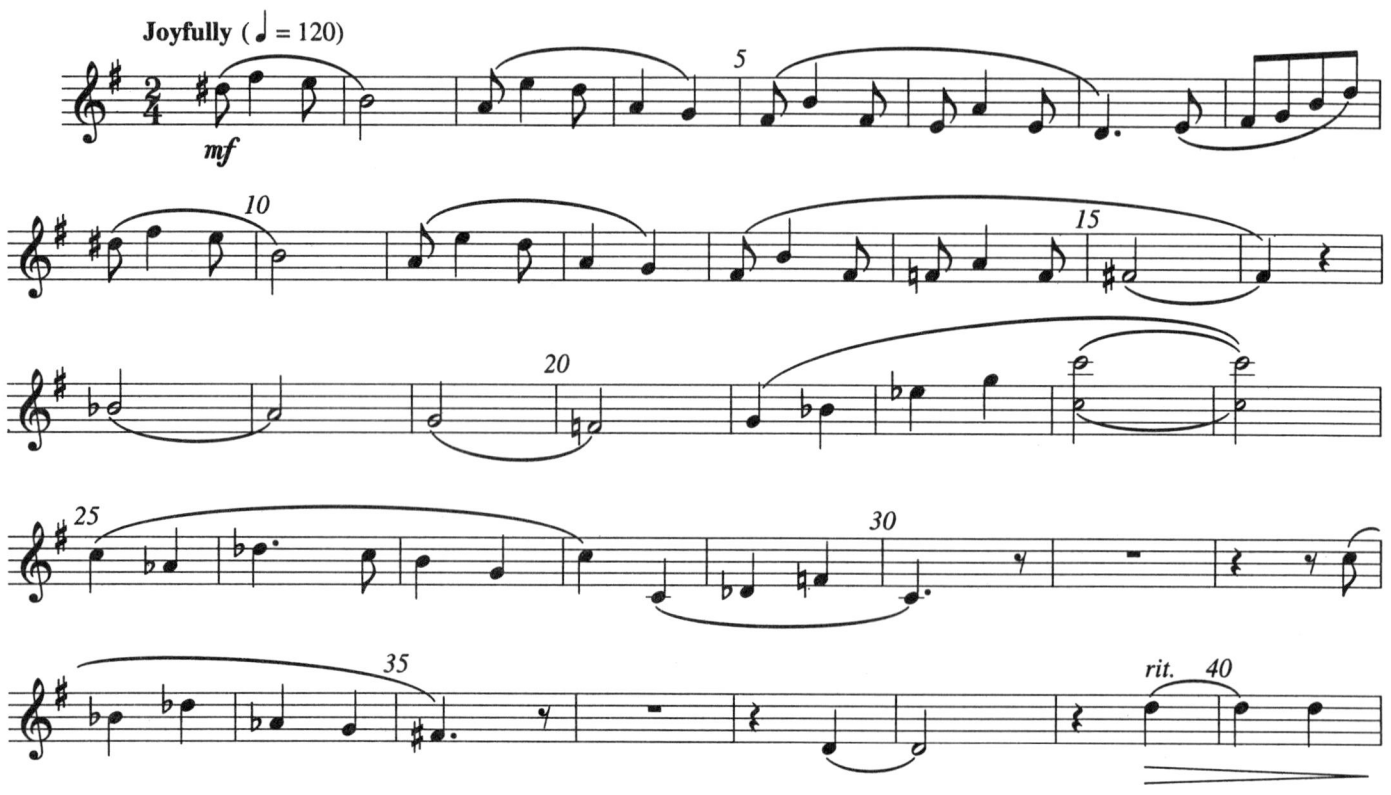

© Copyright 1995 by Kevin Mayhew Ltd.
It is illegal to photocopy music.

BLUES FOR A PINK ELEPHANT

HARRY RABINOWITZ

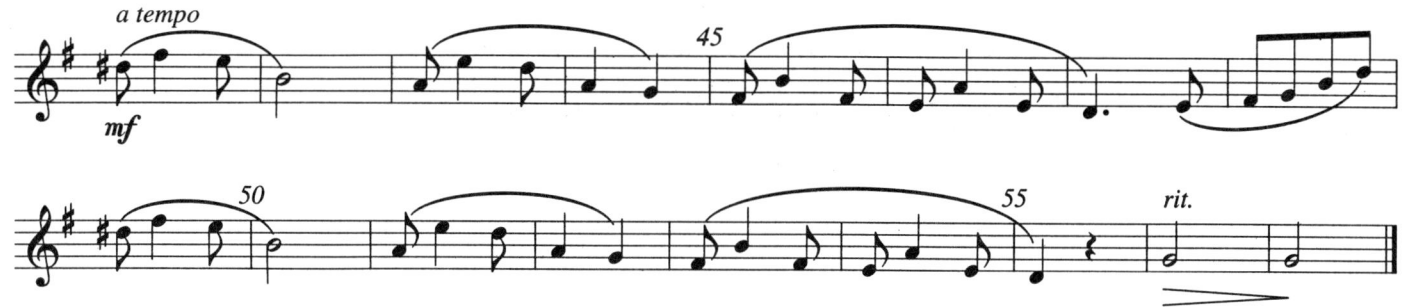

The quavers in this piece should be swung so that ♫ becomes ♩♪ (triplet)

© Copyright 1995 by Kevin Mayhew Ltd.
It is illegal to photocopy music.

For Sarah

HIPPY HABANERA

BETTY ROE

WHAT A SURPRISE

MIKE SAMMES

© Copyright 1995 by Kevin Mayhew Ltd.
It is illegal to photocopy music.

JIM KNOBBLY KNEES

MAX HARRIS

© Copyright 1995 by Kevin Mayhew Ltd.
It is illegal to photocopy music.

MIND THE DOG
MIKE SAMMES

HOT, BUTTERED TOAST
RICHARD LLOYD

© Copyright 1995 by Kevin Mayhew Ltd.
It is illegal to photocopy music.

MARCH OF THE MONKEYS

MALCOLM ARCHER

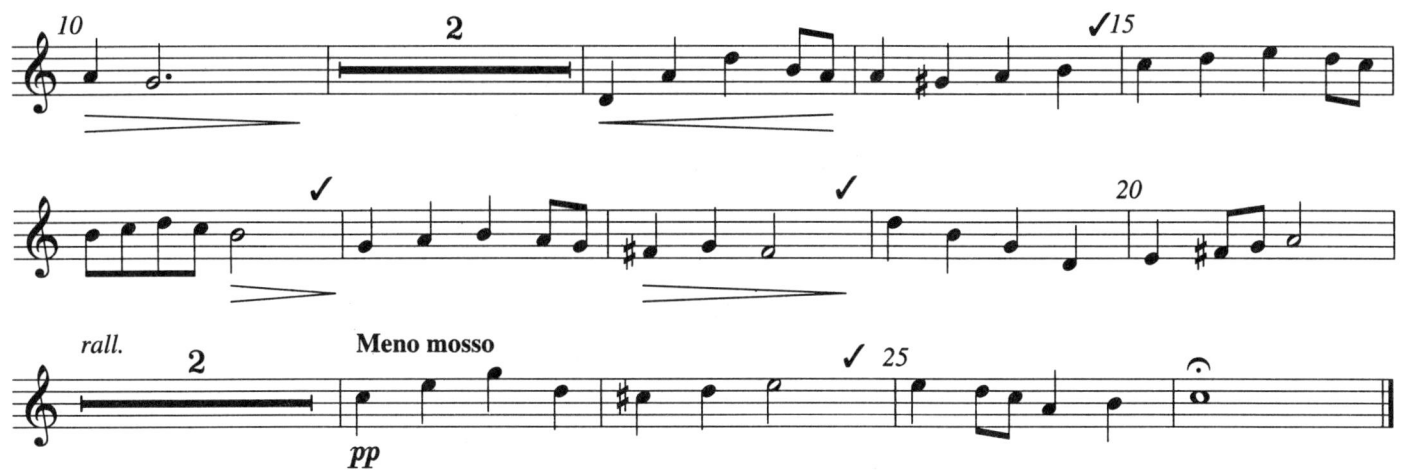

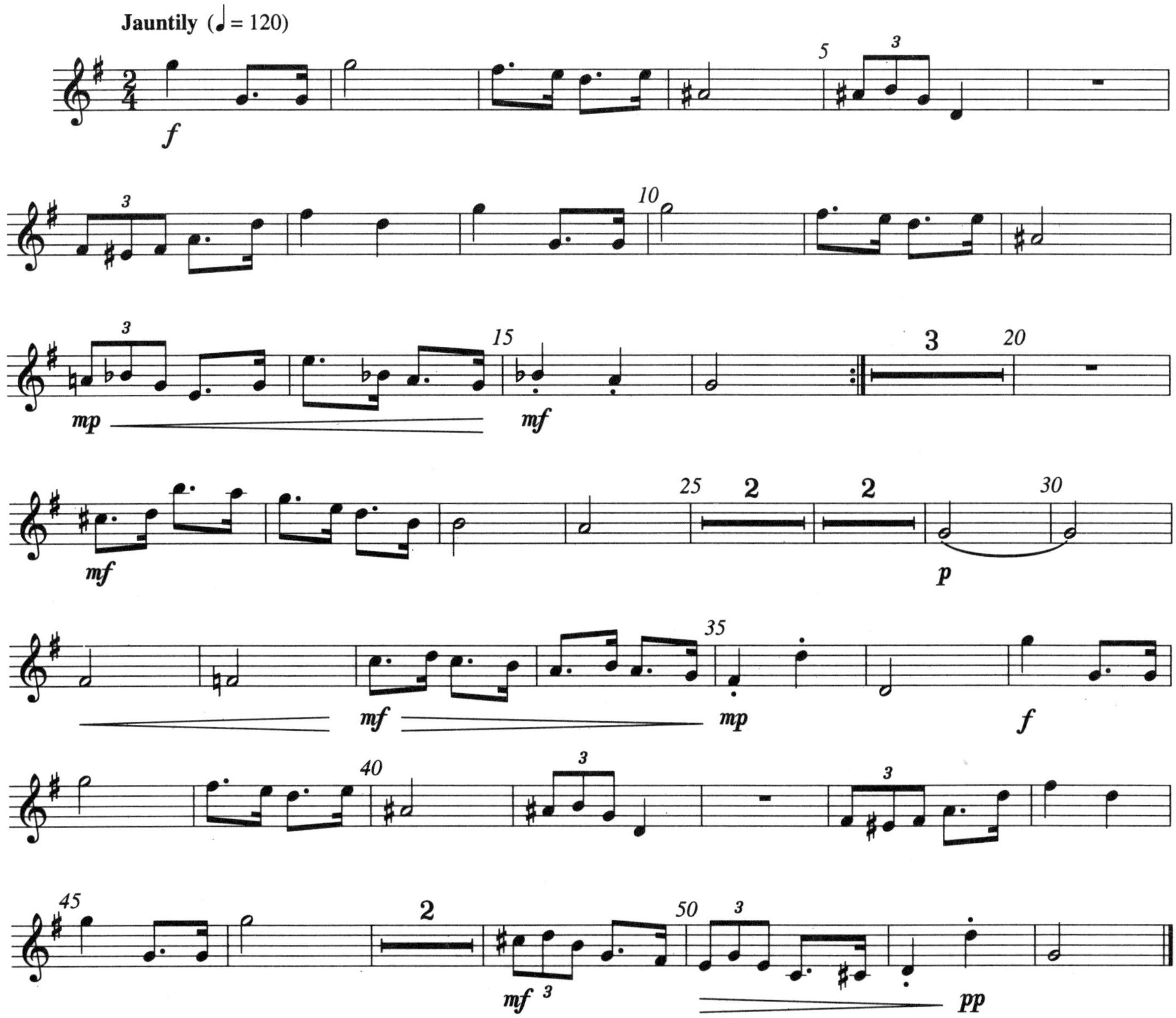

HOW DO YOU DO?

ANDREW MOORE

CHARLIE'S CAKEWALK

BETTY ROE

© Copyright 1995 by Kevin Mayhew Ltd.
It is illegal to photocopy music.

THE ALLIGATOR STOMP

COLIN MAWBY

* This piece should become gradually louder as the alligators get nearer!

JONTY'S JAUNT

NORMAN WARREN

© Copyright 1995 by Kevin Mayhew Ltd.
It is illegal to photocopy music.

LOST LULLABY
ANDREW GANT

© Copyright 1995 by Kevin Mayhew Ltd.
It is illegal to photocopy music.

For Sara

WINDSCREEN WIPER WALTZ

CHRISTOPHER TAMBLING

DAPPER DUKE

JOHN DANKWORTH

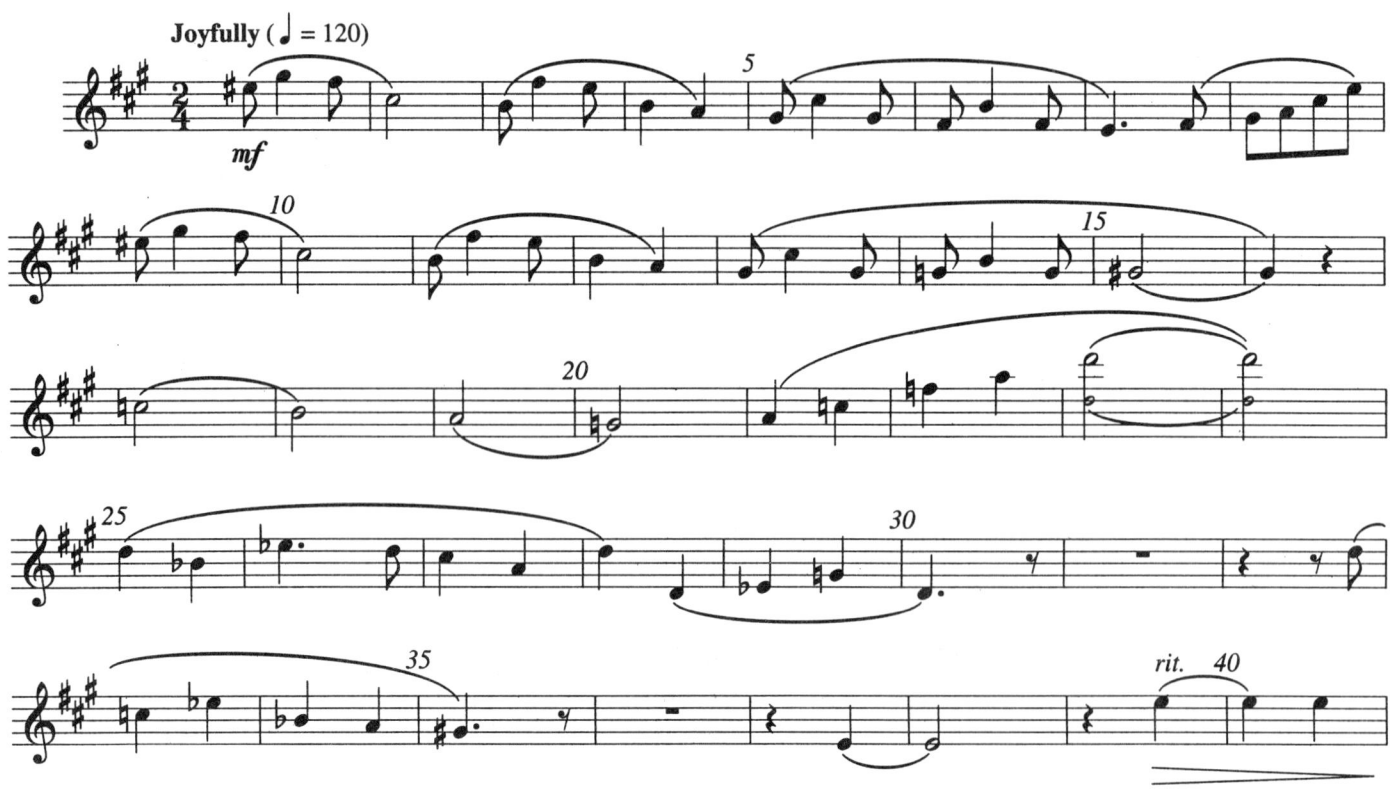

© Copyright 1995 by Kevin Mayhew Ltd.
It is illegal to photocopy music.

BLUES FOR A PINK ELEPHANT

HARRY RABINOWITZ

The quavers in this piece should be swung so that ♫ becomes ♩♪

© Copyright 1995 by Kevin Mayhew Ltd.
It is illegal to photocopy music.

For Sarah

HIPPY HABANERA

BETTY ROE

WHAT A SURPRISE

MIKE SAMMES

© Copyright 1995 by Kevin Mayhew Ltd.
It is illegal to photocopy music.

JIM KNOBBLY KNEES

MAX HARRIS

Slowly and gently

© Copyright 1995 by Kevin Mayhew Ltd.
It is illegal to photocopy music.

MIND THE DOG

MIKE SAMMES

HOT, BUTTERED TOAST

RICHARD LLOYD

© Copyright 1995 by Kevin Mayhew Ltd.
It is illegal to photocopy music.

MARCH OF THE MONKEYS

MALCOLM ARCHER

HOW DO YOU DO?

ANDREW MOORE

CHARLIE'S CAKEWALK

BETTY ROE

© Copyright 1995 by Kevin Mayhew Ltd.
It is illegal to photocopy music.

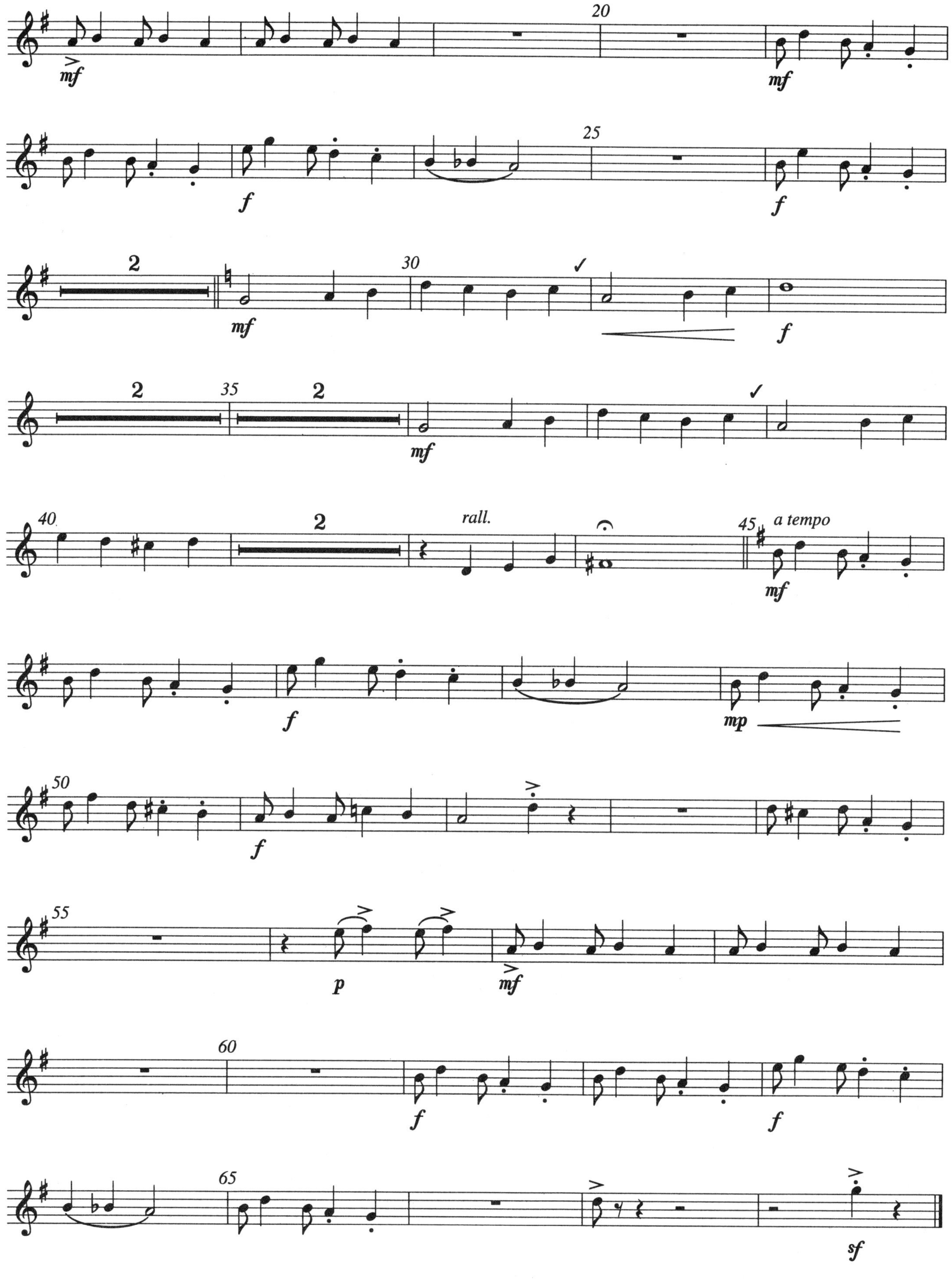
rall.
a tempo

THE ALLIGATOR STOMP

COLIN MAWBY

*This piece should become gradually louder as the alligators get nearer!

JONTY'S JAUNT

NORMAN WARREN

© Copyright 1995 by Kevin Mayhew Ltd.
It is illegal to photocopy music.

LOST LULLABY
ANDREW GANT

Gentle waltz tempo

mp dolce cantabile

© Copyright 1995 by Kevin Mayhew Ltd.
It is illegal to photocopy music.

HOW DO YOU DO?

ANDREW MOORE

Allegro moderato

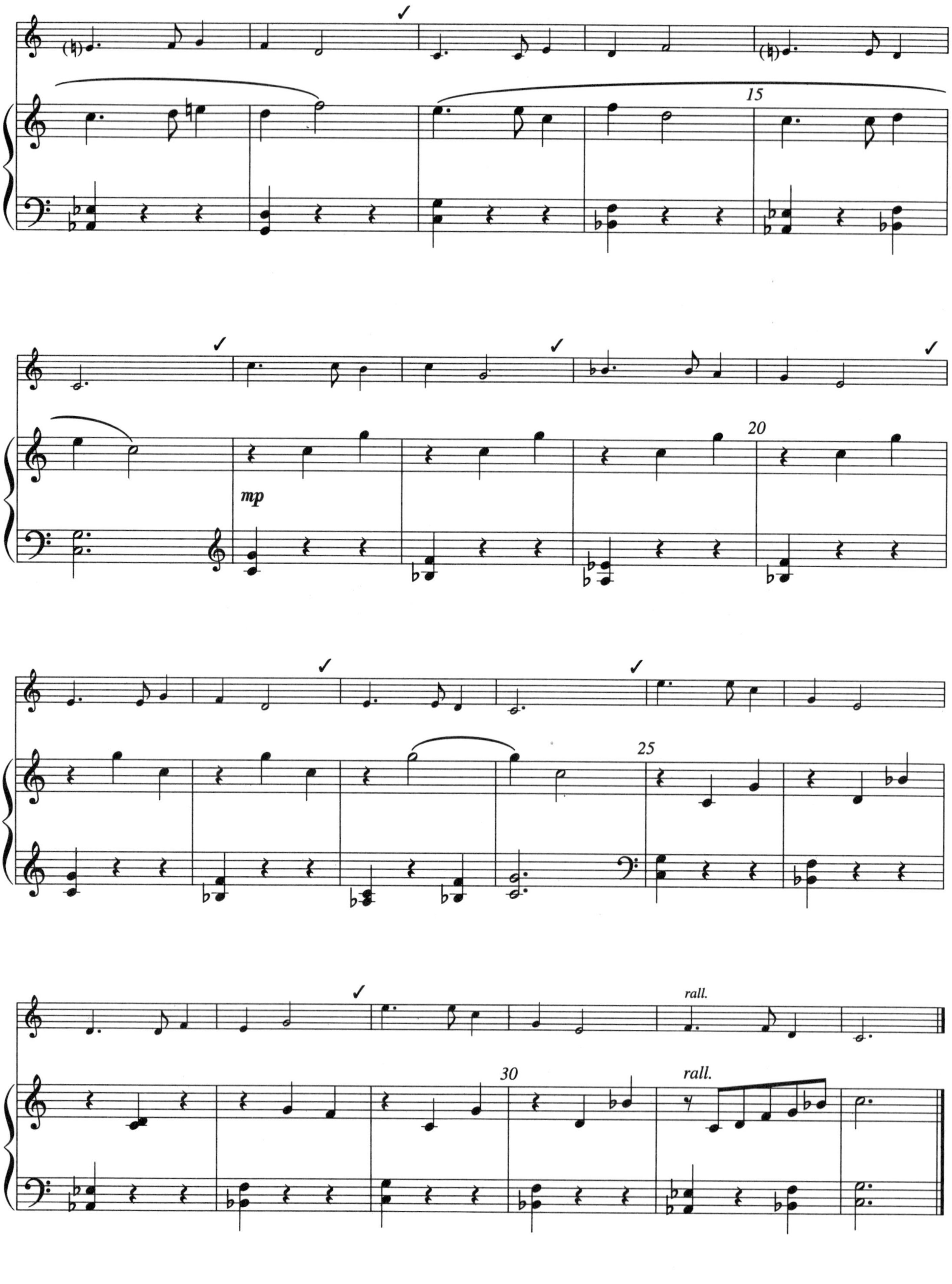

15
mp
20
25
rall.
30
rall.

Charlie's Cakewalk

BETTY ROE

Allegretto

© Copyright 1995 by Kevin Mayhew Ltd.
It is illegal to photocopy music.

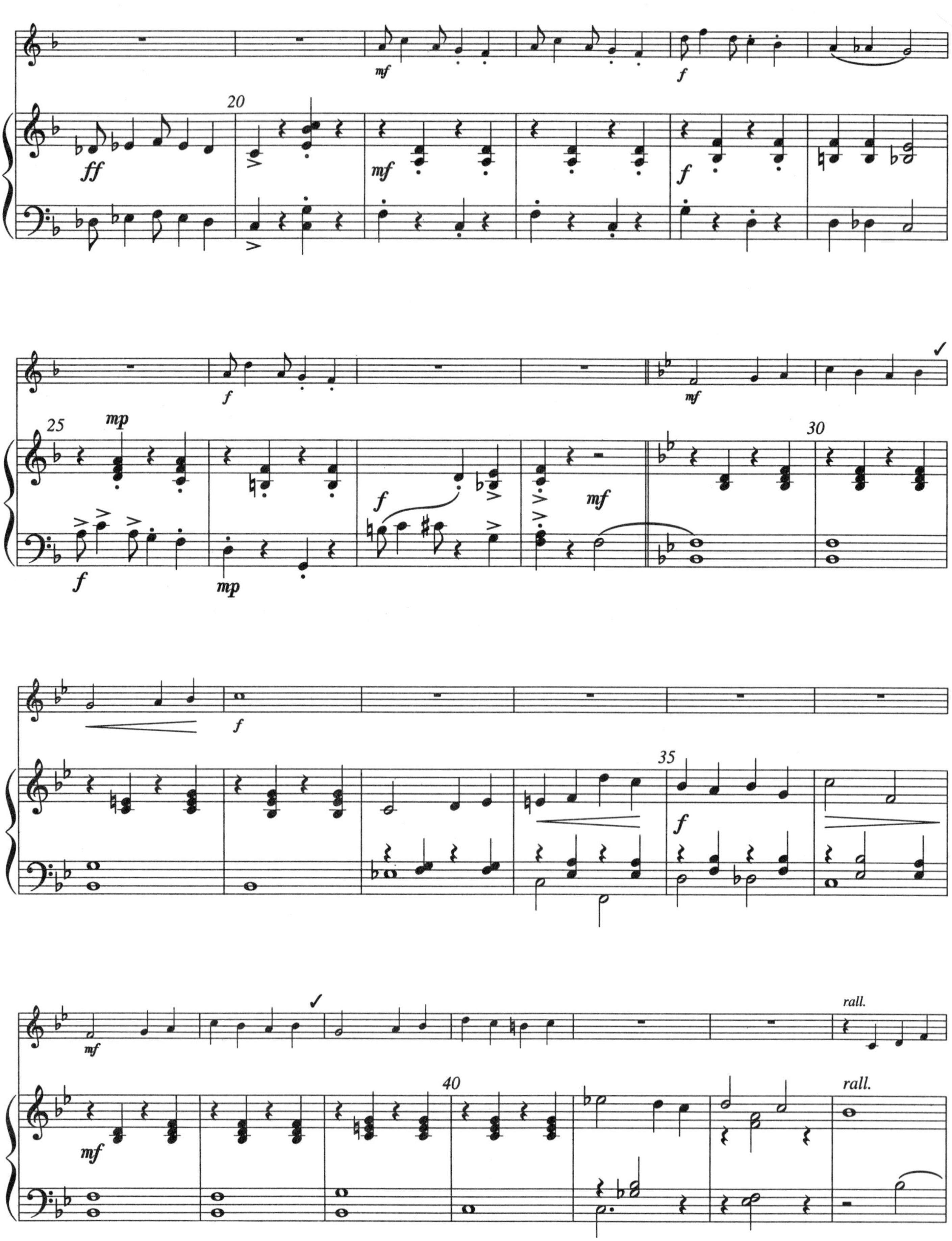
rall.
rall.

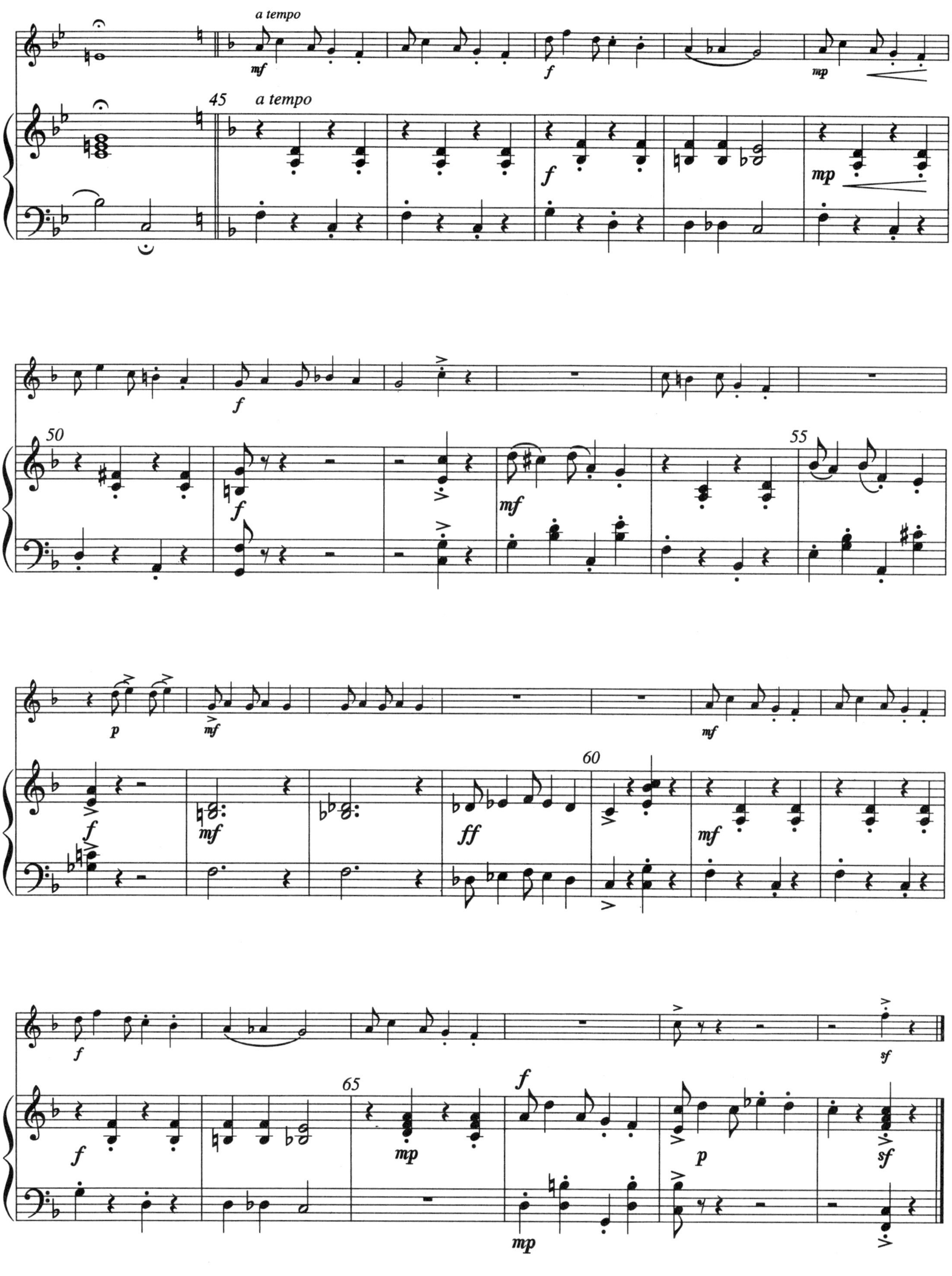
a tempo
45
a tempo
50
55
60
65

THE ALLIGATOR STOMP

COLIN MAWBY

Con brio

mf non legato sempre cresc.   sim.

* This piece should become gradually louder as the alligators get nearer!

© Copyright 1995 by Kevin Mayhew Ltd.
It is illegal to photocopy music.

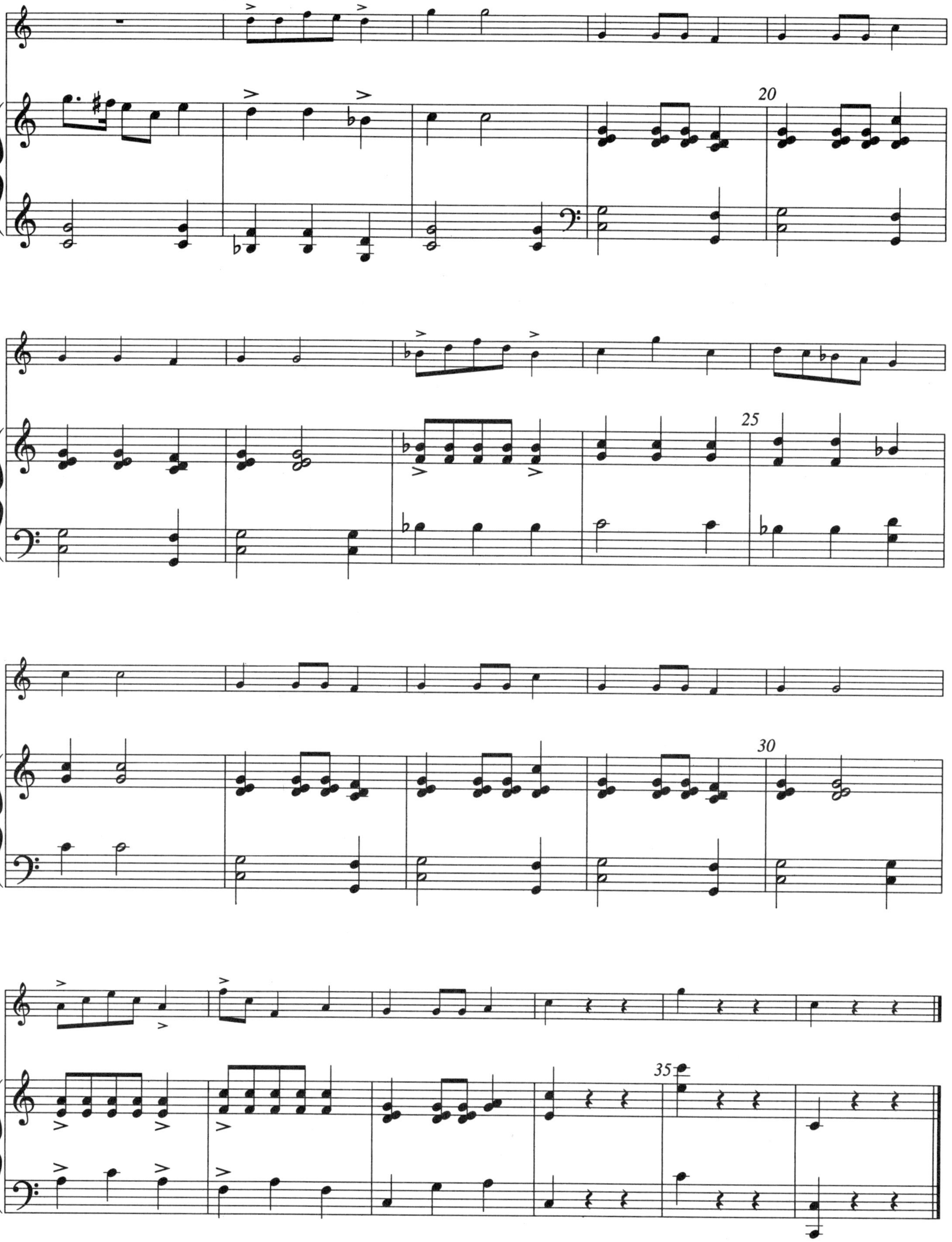
20
25
30
35

JONTY'S JAUNT

NORMAN WARREN

29

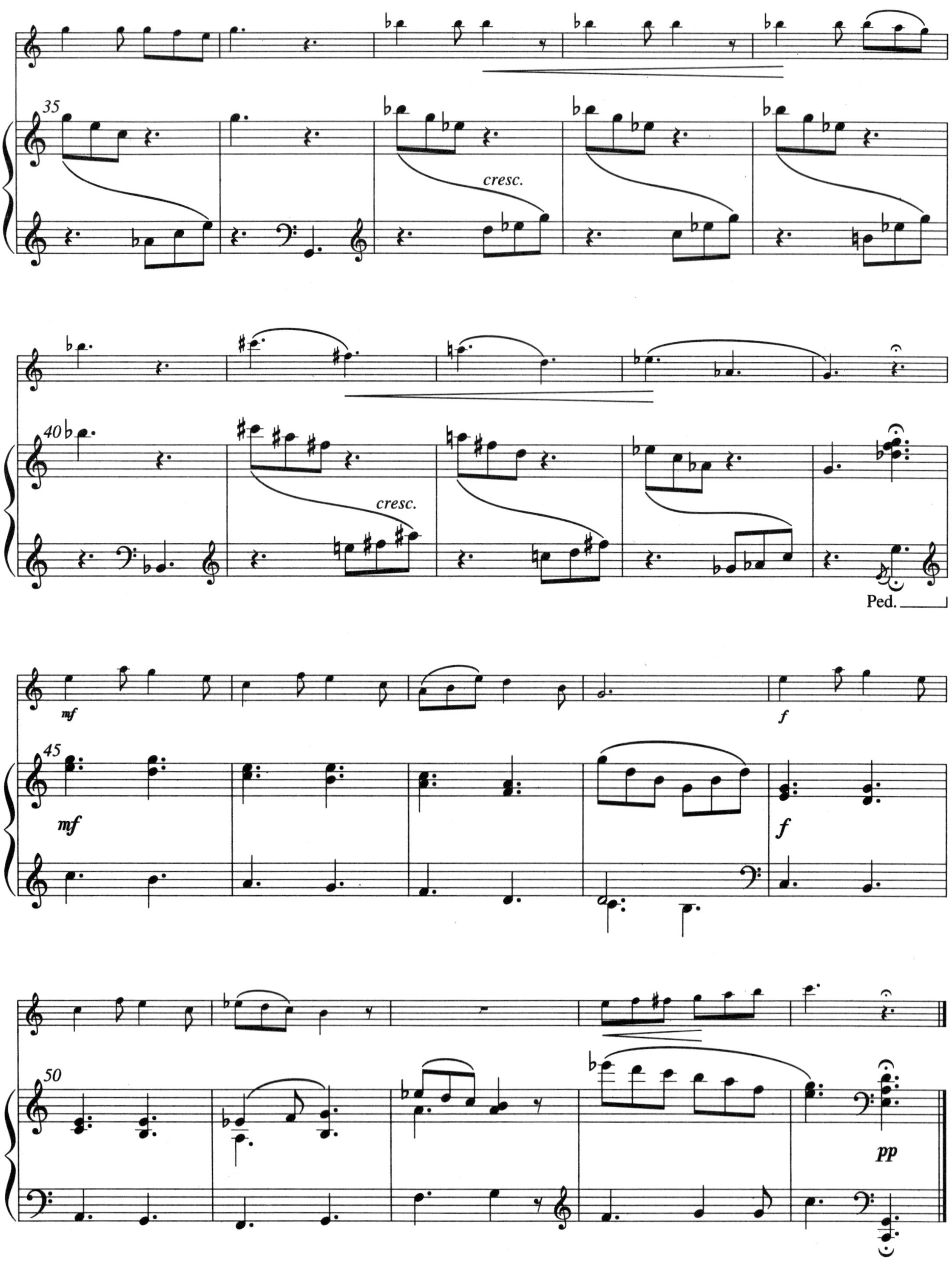
35
cresc.
40
cresc.
Ped.
mf
45
mf
f
f
50
pp

LOST LULLABY
ANDREW GANT